Google AlphaProteo and Orb

The AI Revolution in Protein Design

Designing the Future: Impact on Medicine, Science, and Energy Innovation

Alejandro S. Diego

Table of Contents

Introduction...3

Chapter 1: Understanding Proteins – The Building
Blocks of Life.. 6

Chapter 2: From Prediction to Design – The Birth of
AlphaProteo.. 13

Chapter 3: How AlphaProteo Works – Inside the AI
Engine...22

Chapter 4: Breakthroughs in Drug Discovery –
AlphaProteo's Medical Revolution............................32

Chapter 5: Collaboration for Global Impact –
AlphaProteo's Real-World Applications...................43

Chapter 6: Orb – AI in Material Science................... 56

Chapter 7: Orb's Cutting-Edge Simulation – How It
Works...67

Chapter 8: Open Source Power – Orb's Potential for
Innovation.. 79

Chapter 9: The Bigger Picture – AI's Role in the
Future of Science... 89

Conclusion... 99

Introduction

Artificial intelligence has ushered in an era of unprecedented innovation, touching every corner of science and medicine with its potential to solve complex problems at an accelerated pace. Over the past decade, AI has moved beyond theoretical applications to become a tangible force that is driving change in laboratories, research facilities, and industries across the globe. From revolutionizing how we understand diseases to enhancing the design of life-saving drugs, AI is carving out a critical role in shaping the future of science and medicine. This rapid technological evolution is pushing the boundaries of what was once thought possible.

At the forefront of this transformation are two groundbreaking AI models: Google's AlphaProteo and Orb by Orbital. These technologies represent the next leap in scientific discovery, where AI not only aids in understanding natural processes but actively designs and simulates new possibilities. AlphaProteo has taken the complex task of protein design, something that once took scientists years to accomplish, and condensed it into mere minutes. Proteins, which are the building blocks of life, are now being designed by AI to target specific diseases, opening up new avenues for treatments and breakthroughs in healthcare.

Similarly, Orb is transforming the field of material science. By simulating materials at the atomic level, Orb is making it possible to create more efficient, durable, and sustainable materials for energy solutions like batteries and solar panels. These advancements have the potential to accelerate the global shift toward renewable energy, providing smarter, more effective technologies to power the future.

Together, AlphaProteo and Orb are reshaping not only the future of medicine and science but also the energy sector. As AI continues to evolve, these technologies stand as beacons of what can be achieved when machine learning is applied to some of the most complex challenges we face today. They are not just tools—they are the architects of a new era in discovery, poised to make an indelible mark on the future of innovation.

Chapter 1: Understanding Proteins – The Building Blocks of Life

Proteins are often referred to as the building blocks of life, and for good reason. These complex molecules are essential for nearly every biological process that occurs within living organisms. From the tiniest bacteria to the most complex humans, proteins are responsible for a wide array of functions, making them indispensable to life as we know it. They serve as enzymes that catalyze chemical reactions, structural components that give cells their shape and strength, and messengers that transmit signals between different parts of the body. In short, without proteins, none of the biological functions that sustain life would be possible.

At their core, proteins are made up of long chains of amino acids. The sequence and structure of these amino acids determine the protein's function. Once a protein is formed, it folds into a specific shape that allows it to interact with other molecules, often with incredible precision. These interactions are vital for everything from cellular growth and repair to immune responses and metabolism. Every movement we make, every thought we have, and every breath we take is facilitated by the action of proteins working in perfect harmony.

One of the most critical roles proteins play is in cellular communication. For instance, hormones like insulin are proteins that regulate processes such as blood sugar levels by sending signals to specific cells. Other proteins act as receptors on the surface of cells, receiving signals from hormones or other molecules and triggering specific cellular responses. This constant communication ensures that the body's systems are working together seamlessly.

Proteins also play a vital role in our immune systems. Antibodies, for example, are proteins designed to recognize and bind to foreign invaders like bacteria and viruses, marking them for destruction. Without this protein-based defense mechanism, our bodies would be vulnerable to countless diseases.

Given their immense importance, understanding how proteins interact with each other and the molecules around them has been a central focus of scientific research for decades. This knowledge is key to advancing medicine, as many diseases result from protein malfunctions or misfolding. The ability to design proteins that can correct these issues or target specific disease-causing agents has long been a goal in fields like drug discovery and biotechnology.

As we unlock the secrets of how proteins function and interact, we open the door to transformative medical and scientific breakthroughs. This is where artificial intelligence steps in, accelerating our ability to analyze, predict, and design proteins that could one day offer cures for diseases or improve our quality of life.

Understanding how proteins interact with each other and with other molecules is one of the most challenging aspects of biology. Proteins rarely act in isolation; instead, they interact in highly specific ways that dictate the outcome of many vital processes within living organisms. These interactions are akin to intricate puzzles, where the shape, structure, and chemical properties of each protein determine how well they can bind and communicate with others. The precise nature of these interactions is critical because even a slight change can have significant consequences, leading to diseases or health disorders.

For example, when proteins misfold or interact incorrectly, it can lead to conditions like Alzheimer's, cystic fibrosis, or certain cancers. These diseases are often the result of a single error in protein interaction, which disrupts the normal functioning of cells. Scientists have long recognized that if we could fully understand and predict how proteins interact, we could develop more effective treatments for these conditions. However, given the immense complexity of proteins and the nearly infinite number of ways they can fold and interact, this task has proven incredibly difficult.

Traditional methods of studying protein interactions, such as X-ray crystallography and nuclear magnetic resonance (NMR) spectroscopy, are time-consuming and expensive. These approaches require years of research to decipher just a single protein structure. The challenge has been not only to understand how one protein functions but also to predict how it will interact with other proteins, molecules, or potential drugs. This has been a significant bottleneck in fields like drug discovery, where understanding these interactions could lead to the development of treatments for a wide array of diseases.

This is where artificial intelligence, particularly Google's AlphaFold, has changed the game.

AlphaFold, developed by DeepMind, represents a major breakthrough in the field of protein prediction. For decades, scientists sought ways to predict the 3D structure of proteins based solely on their amino acid sequences, a challenge known as the "protein folding problem." AlphaFold achieved remarkable success in this area, using machine learning to predict protein structures with astonishing accuracy. In 2020, AlphaFold's performance in the Critical Assessment of Structure Prediction (CASP) competition stunned the scientific community, as it was able to predict the 3D structures of proteins at a level of accuracy comparable to experimental methods.

AlphaFold's ability to predict protein structures has provided researchers with invaluable insights into how proteins fold and interact, accelerating discoveries in biology and medicine. By understanding the shapes of proteins, scientists can more effectively design drugs that bind to these proteins, potentially inhibiting harmful interactions or restoring normal function in diseased cells. AlphaFold has already been used to make advances in understanding diseases like COVID-19 and has applications in countless other areas of science.

While AlphaFold has revolutionized protein prediction, it is just the beginning. The next leap forward comes from AI systems like AlphaProteo, which don't just predict how proteins will fold but actively design new proteins to influence specific interactions. This ability to design custom proteins holds enormous potential for the future of medicine and health, allowing scientists to address diseases at their molecular root.

Chapter 2: From Prediction to Design – The Birth of AlphaProteo

While AlphaFold brought a transformative change to how we understand protein structures by accurately predicting how proteins fold, AlphaProteo takes this breakthrough even further. AlphaFold's major achievement was in prediction—helping scientists visualize how proteins take on their complex 3D shapes, which is crucial for understanding their function. However, it had limitations. AlphaFold could show us how proteins exist in their natural form, but it couldn't create new proteins that might help tackle specific diseases or solve other biological challenges.

This is where AlphaProteo steps in, representing a leap from passive prediction to active design. AlphaProteo doesn't just predict protein structures; it designs entirely new proteins tailored to bind to specific molecular targets. This ability moves beyond the realm of understanding nature as it is, enabling scientists to engineer nature as it could be. It's like the difference between observing a lock and having the ability to craft a custom key to fit perfectly into that lock, designed to unlock specific biological pathways or block disease-causing mechanisms.

One of the most significant areas where AlphaProteo shines is in drug discovery and biomedical research. Traditional methods of designing proteins that bind to target molecules, such as those involved in diseases like cancer or viral infections, have been painstakingly slow. Scientists have typically relied on trial-and-error processes, spending years or even decades to develop protein binders that work efficiently. The design process requires synthesizing proteins in the lab, testing them, optimizing the design, and then repeating the process to improve results.

With AlphaProteo, this timeline is drastically shortened. By training on vast datasets, including millions of protein structures and interactions, AlphaProteo can design proteins that fit target molecules almost perfectly on the first attempt. This capability means that researchers no longer need to go through countless iterations of trial and error. The AI system rapidly generates high-quality protein designs that can be tested in labs, accelerating the entire process of drug development and medical research.

AlphaProteo's capacity to design proteins with specific functions has applications across various fields. For example, it has been used to develop protein binders for viral proteins, such as those from SARS-CoV-2, the virus responsible for COVID-19. By designing proteins that bind to and neutralize the virus, AlphaProteo offers a new tool in the fight against infectious diseases. Beyond viruses, the AI system has been used to target proteins linked to cancer, autoimmune disorders, and other complex conditions, offering new hope for treatments that are more effective and precisely targeted.

In addition to healthcare, AlphaProteo's protein-design capabilities extend to agriculture, where it is being explored to create proteins that can enhance crop resistance to pests or improve nutritional content. The implications of this technology are vast, providing new ways to tackle some of the world's most pressing challenges in medicine, food security, and beyond.

AlphaProteo builds upon the foundations laid by AlphaFold, taking protein research from a tool that helps us understand biology to one that allows us to reshape it. This leap from prediction to design is one of the most exciting developments in AI-driven science, offering the potential to engineer new solutions to problems that were previously out of reach.

AlphaProteo marks a significant evolution in the application of AI to biology by shifting from merely predicting how proteins fold to actively designing new proteins with specific functions. At the core of this leap is the idea that proteins are not just static components of biology, but can be custom-engineered to solve a variety of challenges across medicine, agriculture, and beyond. AlphaProteo's ability to create new proteins tailored to bind to specific molecules unlocks a host of new possibilities in scientific research and practical applications.

The process begins with the vast amount of data AlphaProteo has been trained on. Using information from the Protein Data Bank and over 100 million protein structures predicted by AlphaFold, AlphaProteo has learned the rules of how proteins interact at a molecular level. These interactions, which are fundamental to biological processes, are often compared to a key fitting into a lock. The "key" is a protein, and the "lock" is a target molecule—such as a virus, a cancer cell, or a pest-resistance factor in plants. The precision with which a protein binds to its target determines its effectiveness in triggering, blocking, or modifying a biological function.

What sets AlphaProteo apart is its ability to not only understand these existing interactions but to design proteins that fit perfectly into specific molecular targets. This process, which previously took years of laboratory work, can now be done in a fraction of the time. Scientists can input the structure of a target protein—say, a viral spike protein from SARS-CoV-2—and instruct AlphaProteo to create a new protein that binds tightly to this target. In essence, AlphaProteo is given the blueprint of a lock, and it designs the perfect key.

These newly designed proteins, known as **binders**, have a wide array of applications. In medicine, they can be used to develop new treatments by targeting disease-causing proteins more precisely than ever before. For example, in cancer research, AlphaProteo has been used to create protein binders that can attach to cancer-related proteins and disrupt their ability to spread or grow, potentially leading to new therapies. In the case of viral infections like COVID-19, binders designed by AlphaProteo can neutralize the virus by blocking its ability to infect cells. The potential to design proteins that target specific disease mechanisms opens up new avenues for therapeutic development, offering a powerful tool for fighting everything from infectious diseases to chronic conditions like autoimmune disorders.

Beyond medicine, the concept of protein binders extends into agriculture. AlphaProteo's capabilities can be harnessed to create proteins that improve plant resilience against pests and diseases, potentially reducing the need for harmful pesticides or genetic modification. By designing proteins that enhance the natural defenses of crops, AlphaProteo could play a significant role in improving food security and sustainability. Additionally, the same principles can be applied to improve the nutritional content of plants or to engineer crops that are more resistant to environmental stressors, such as drought or extreme temperatures.

The ability to create new proteins with such precision has also been transformative for fundamental biological research. Scientists now have the tools to explore previously uncharted territories of biology, where custom-designed proteins can be used to study complex processes at a molecular level. This new frontier of protein design allows for more sophisticated experiments, leading to deeper insights into how diseases develop and how biological systems function.

AlphaProteo's creation of new proteins is a game-changer, not just because it accelerates research, but because it enables solutions that were once unimaginable. By designing binders tailored to specific targets, this AI system offers the potential to revolutionize fields as diverse as drug discovery, agriculture, and even bioengineering. The implications are profound: AlphaProteo is giving scientists the ability to create molecular tools that could one day provide cures for diseases, improve the resilience of food systems, and unlock new levels of understanding in biology.

Chapter 3: How AlphaProteo Works – Inside the AI Engine

AlphaProteo's AI engine is an advanced system built upon the principles of machine learning, specifically designed to tackle one of biology's most complex challenges: creating custom proteins that bind to specific molecular targets. This AI engine draws from an enormous amount of data and uses sophisticated algorithms to design proteins that can perform specific functions, revolutionizing the fields of medicine, agriculture, and beyond.

At the heart of AlphaProteo's power is the data it has been trained on. It uses two main sources of information: the **Protein Data Bank (PDB)** and **AlphaFold's 100 million predicted protein structures**. The Protein Data Bank is a comprehensive repository that contains decades of research on experimentally determined protein structures. This gives AlphaProteo a solid foundation of real-world biological data to work from. Meanwhile, AlphaFold, which made a groundbreaking contribution by predicting the 3D structures of proteins based on their amino acid sequences, has generated a vast library of protein predictions. With access to over 100 million predicted structures, AlphaProteo has been exposed to an incredible variety of proteins, learning how they fold, interact, and function.

The AI engine processes this massive amount of data and applies machine learning techniques to identify patterns in protein interactions. By analyzing how proteins naturally bind to other molecules, AlphaProteo learns the underlying rules that govern these interactions. This knowledge is critical when it comes to designing new proteins that can bind to specific targets. Essentially, the AI is learning what makes a protein a good "key" to fit a particular molecular "lock."

The process begins when scientists input the structure of a target protein, which could be anything from a viral protein to a protein associated with cancer. The goal is to design a new protein, known as a **binder**, that will attach to this target with precision. The AI uses the lock and key analogy to guide its design process. Imagine the target protein as a lock that needs to be unlocked or blocked, depending on the desired outcome. AlphaProteo's job is to design the perfect key that will fit into this lock and alter its behavior. The key (or binder) must be shaped in just the right way to interact with the target protein, ensuring it binds tightly and effectively.

AlphaProteo's AI engine takes into account the shape, charge, and chemical properties of the target protein. It then generates thousands of potential binders that could theoretically fit the target. This is where AlphaProteo's power comes into play: instead of manually testing each of these binders in the lab—a process that would take years—the AI rapidly evaluates them through simulation. Using its learned knowledge from the protein data bank and AlphaFold's predictions, AlphaProteo can predict how each of these binders will interact with the target protein. The AI ranks the best candidates based on their predicted effectiveness, narrowing down the options to a handful of highly optimized binders that are ready for laboratory testing.

Once these potential binders are selected, they are synthesized and tested in real-world experiments. The accuracy of AlphaProteo's predictions has been remarkable, often producing binders that work far better than those designed by traditional methods. In some cases, AlphaProteo's binders have been shown to bind to target proteins with binding strengths that are up to 300 times better than previously available designs. This leap in efficiency and precision is a testament to the sophistication of the AI engine, which combines data-driven insights with real-world applicability.

This lock and key approach is not only elegant but also highly versatile. AlphaProteo can be used to design proteins for a wide range of applications. In medicine, it can create binders that neutralize disease-causing proteins, offering new treatment options for conditions like cancer, autoimmune disorders, and viral infections. In agriculture, it can design proteins that enhance the resistance of crops to pests or environmental stressors. The potential applications are vast, and AlphaProteo's AI engine is driving innovation across multiple fields by enabling scientists to engineer proteins with unprecedented speed and accuracy.

AlphaProteo's ability to learn from an immense dataset and apply this knowledge to design proteins tailored to specific molecular targets marks a profound shift in how science approaches protein design. This AI engine is not just speeding up research—it is fundamentally changing how we solve biological problems by giving us the tools to create custom solutions at the molecular level.

AlphaProteo's ability to design binders for specific proteins has opened up new avenues for practical applications in medicine, particularly in addressing some of the most pressing health challenges we face today. One of the standout features of this AI system is its capacity to target proteins associated with diseases like COVID-19, cancer, and autoimmune disorders. These diseases often hinge on protein interactions that either promote the spread of disease or interfere with the body's normal functions. By designing binders that can precisely target these proteins, AlphaProteo offers new potential for treatments that are more effective, specific, and faster to develop than traditional methods.

In the case of **COVID-19**, one of the key proteins involved is the spike protein of the SARS-CoV-2 virus. This spike protein plays a critical role in how the virus attaches to and enters human cells, initiating infection. Traditional approaches to combating the virus have included vaccines and therapeutics aimed at disrupting this interaction. AlphaProteo, however, provides a more direct and powerful tool by designing protein binders that can latch onto the spike protein, effectively neutralizing its ability to infect cells. These binders act as molecular blockers, preventing the virus from using its spike protein to penetrate the cell membrane. The AI-designed binders have been tested in laboratories, and some have shown remarkable success, not only in blocking the original SARS-CoV-2 virus but also in tackling its variants, which have posed ongoing challenges in the fight against the pandemic. This rapid ability to adapt and design binders for evolving viral threats underscores the power of AlphaProteo in combating infectious diseases.

When it comes to **cancer**, the stakes are equally high. Cancer is often driven by abnormal proteins that either stimulate unchecked cell growth or prevent the body's natural mechanisms from halting the spread of malignant cells. AlphaProteo has been used to design binders that target these rogue proteins, disrupting their harmful interactions and providing a new approach to cancer therapy. For instance, AlphaProteo has successfully designed binders for proteins like V GFA (Vascular Endothelial Growth Factor A), a protein that plays a significant role in tumor growth by promoting the formation of new blood vessels (a process called angiogenesis). By binding to V GFA, the designed proteins can effectively block this process, starving the tumor of the nutrients it needs to grow. This kind of targeted therapy offers the potential to treat cancer more precisely, reducing the side effects that often come with traditional treatments like chemotherapy, which can harm healthy cells as well as cancerous ones.

In the field of **autoimmune diseases**, AlphaProteo's binders are equally promising. Autoimmune diseases occur when the body's immune system mistakenly attacks its own cells, often because of malfunctioning proteins that trigger an inappropriate immune response. One of the key proteins involved in autoimmune conditions like rheumatoid arthritis is TNFα (Tumor Necrosis Factor alpha), which promotes inflammation and contributes to the damage of healthy tissues. Traditional treatments for autoimmune diseases often aim to suppress the immune system broadly, which can lead to a range of unwanted side effects and leave the patient vulnerable to infections. AlphaProteo, however, can design binders that specifically target TNFα, neutralizing its harmful effects without broadly suppressing the immune system. Although the design of binders for particularly challenging proteins like TNFα is still evolving, early results show great potential for creating more focused therapies that could transform how autoimmune diseases are treated.

These practical applications demonstrate the versatility and precision of AlphaProteo. In each case—whether it's targeting a viral protein like SARS-CoV-2's spike protein, disrupting cancer-promoting proteins, or neutralizing the inflammatory proteins that drive autoimmune diseases—AlphaProteo's binders are designed with surgical precision. They bind only to the targeted proteins, minimizing off-target effects and reducing the chances of harmful side effects, a major advantage over many existing treatments. Moreover, the speed at which AlphaProteo can generate these binders, combined with its ability to refine them based on ongoing research, makes it a powerful tool for responding to both current and emerging health crises.

In summary, AlphaProteo's practical applications in medicine are reshaping the landscape of treatment for diseases like COVID-19, cancer, and autoimmune disorders. By offering a faster, more precise method of designing protein binders, AlphaProteo is providing scientists and clinicians with new ways to combat these complex diseases, opening the door to more effective therapies and potentially life-saving interventions.

Chapter 4: Breakthroughs in Drug Discovery – AlphaProteo's Medical Revolution

AlphaProteo's groundbreaking technology has already yielded impressive results in several key areas of medical research, with some remarkable case studies that highlight its potential. These case studies illustrate how the AI system has successfully designed protein binders for critical proteins associated with diseases like COVID-19 and cancer, while also shedding light on the challenges that remain, particularly in the realm of autoimmune diseases.

One of the most significant early successes of AlphaProteo has been in the fight against **COVID-19**. The virus responsible for the global pandemic, SARS-CoV-2, relies heavily on its spike protein to infect human cells. This spike protein binds to receptors on the surface of human cells, allowing the virus to enter and replicate, which is the key step in viral infection. Traditional treatments and vaccines target this spike protein, aiming to neutralize it before the virus can establish an infection. AlphaProteo took this challenge a step further by designing protein binders that could latch onto the spike protein more effectively than naturally occurring molecules or antibodies.

In laboratory tests, these binders demonstrated a strong ability to block the spike protein, preventing the virus from attaching to human cells. What's even more impressive is that AlphaProteo was able to design binders for not only the original SARS-CoV-2 spike protein but also its variants, which have been responsible for multiple waves of infection during the pandemic. This flexibility and speed in adapting to new viral mutations show how AI-designed proteins can be an essential tool in fighting fast-evolving viral threats. The implications for virus prevention are enormous: AlphaProteo's protein binders could potentially be developed into therapeutic treatments that stop the virus from infecting cells altogether, providing an additional line of defense alongside vaccines and antiviral drugs.

In the field of **cancer research**, AlphaProteo has made significant strides by designing protein binders for cancer-related proteins. One of the most successful applications has been in targeting **Vascular Endothelial Growth Factor A (V GFA)**, a protein that is critical to the process of angiogenesis, where tumors stimulate the growth of new blood vessels to supply themselves with nutrients. Cancer treatments often aim to block this process, as cutting off the blood supply can starve the tumor and inhibit its growth. Traditional therapies targeting V GFA, such as monoclonal antibodies, have had some success, but there has always been room for improvement in terms of binding efficiency and specificity.

AlphaProteo tackled this challenge by designing binders specifically for V GFA that could disrupt its role in angiogenesis. The results have been promising, with some of the designed binders showing up to 300 times stronger binding affinity than existing treatments. This increased binding strength could translate to more effective cancer therapies, as stronger and more specific binders would be better able to block V GFA's activity, potentially slowing or halting tumor growth more efficiently than current methods. Moreover, the precision of these binders reduces the likelihood of off-target effects, a common issue with traditional cancer therapies, making treatment potentially safer and more tolerable for patients.

While AlphaProteo's successes in COVID-19 and cancer research are significant, it has also faced challenges that highlight the complexity of certain diseases, particularly **autoimmune disorders**. One of the toughest targets AlphaProteo has worked on is **Tumor Necrosis Factor alpha (TNFα)**, a protein deeply involved in inflammation and autoimmune conditions like rheumatoid arthritis. TNFα promotes inflammation by binding to receptors on immune cells, triggering a cascade of immune responses. In autoimmune diseases, this process becomes overactive, leading the immune system to attack healthy tissues.

Designing protein binders for TNFα has proven particularly difficult. The protein itself is a complex target, known to be resistant to many forms of treatment. While AlphaProteo has made strides in generating candidate binders, the results have not been as consistently successful as those seen with other proteins. TNFα's role in the immune system is highly dynamic, making it a challenging molecule to bind effectively without disrupting other critical immune functions. However, these challenges are driving further innovations in AlphaProteo's design processes. The team is pushing the limits of the system, learning from each attempt, and using this knowledge to improve the AI's capabilities in targeting such difficult proteins. The difficulties with TNFα highlight the need for continued development and refinement of AI-driven protein design, particularly when tackling proteins that are central to complex diseases like autoimmune disorders.

These case studies illustrate both the remarkable potential and the ongoing challenges of AlphaProteo's technology. Its ability to design highly effective protein binders for COVID-19 and cancer has demonstrated that AI can accelerate medical breakthroughs and offer new hope in disease treatment. Meanwhile, the challenges posed by proteins like TNFα underscore that while the technology is advancing rapidly, there is still much to learn. As AlphaProteo continues to evolve, it is poised to overcome these hurdles, further pushing the boundaries of what is possible in medicine and disease research.

AlphaProteo is revolutionizing drug development by significantly reducing the time and effort required to design and test new treatments. Traditional drug development is a lengthy, labor-intensive process that involves years of research, trial, and error. Researchers typically begin by identifying potential drug targets—often specific proteins or molecules involved in a disease process. Once a target is identified, scientists work to design a drug that can interact with it effectively, often through complex and repetitive testing cycles to refine the drug's efficacy and safety.

In contrast, AlphaProteo dramatically accelerates this process by leveraging AI to design proteins, known as binders, that target disease-related proteins with a precision and speed that far exceeds human capability. Instead of relying on years of laboratory experiments to find a suitable drug candidate, AlphaProteo can quickly generate multiple potential binders for a specific protein, simulating how they will interact with the target.

This process significantly reduces the need for trial and error because the AI has already optimized these designs based on millions of protein interactions it has analyzed and learned from.

AlphaProteo's ability to predict how proteins will bind to targets in silico (via computer simulation) means that researchers can bypass much of the initial experimental phase. In a matter of minutes, AlphaProteo generates highly effective protein designs that can be tested in labs. This marks a major departure from traditional methods, which often require scientists to manually create, test, and refine binders through laborious, time-consuming processes. The efficiency of AlphaProteo not only saves time but also reduces costs, as fewer physical experiments are required, and the likelihood of success with the first batch of designed proteins is far higher.

For example, in the case of a disease like cancer, where certain proteins are involved in tumor growth, AlphaProteo can quickly design a protein binder that targets these proteins with high specificity. The AI evaluates how tightly and effectively the binder will attach to the cancer-related protein, allowing researchers to focus on testing the most promising candidates in real-world conditions. This means that the timeline from initial discovery to potential treatment can be drastically shortened—what used to take years can now be accomplished in months or even weeks.

Moreover, AlphaProteo's AI-driven approach allows for rapid iteration. If an initial design is not effective or needs further optimization, AlphaProteo can quickly generate new binders, learning from previous results and improving the design. This adaptability is particularly important in rapidly evolving fields like virology or oncology, where time is critical, and the need to develop effective treatments quickly is paramount.

AlphaProteo also plays a crucial role in addressing emerging health threats, such as viral pandemics. During the COVID-19 pandemic, one of the major challenges in drug development was the need to quickly respond to new variants of the virus. AlphaProteo's speed in designing binders for the spike protein of SARS-CoV-2 allowed researchers to keep pace with the virus as it mutated, offering new avenues for therapeutic intervention. This ability to rapidly adapt and design treatments for evolving pathogens represents a paradigm shift in how the pharmaceutical industry can respond to global health crises.

In addition to its speed, AlphaProteo improves the overall accuracy of drug development. Traditional methods often result in drugs that interact with unintended targets, leading to side effects or diminished efficacy. AlphaProteo's AI ensures that the binders it designs are highly specific, reducing the risk of off-target effects and increasing the likelihood that the resulting treatment will be both safe and effective. This level of precision not only speeds up the process but also increases the success rate of new drugs, as fewer candidates fail during clinical trials due to unforeseen complications.

By combining rapid design, high precision, and the ability to adapt quickly to new challenges, AlphaProteo is transforming the landscape of drug development. Its ability to generate optimized protein binders in record time allows scientists to focus their efforts on testing and refining the most promising candidates, speeding up the journey from the laboratory to the clinic. This shift in the drug development paradigm has the potential to save countless lives, offering new hope for patients with diseases that currently have limited treatment options, and enabling a faster response to future global health emergencies.

Chapter 5: Collaboration for Global Impact – AlphaProteo's Real-World Applications

AlphaProteo's groundbreaking technology has not only garnered attention for its ability to design new proteins, but it has also attracted collaborations with leading research institutions like the **Francis Crick Institute** and other prominent groups around the world. These partnerships play a crucial role in validating and applying the AI's innovations to real-world challenges in medicine and science. By collaborating with experts in biochemistry, molecular biology, and drug discovery, AlphaProteo's creators are ensuring that the AI's designed proteins are tested rigorously and translated into tangible outcomes that can make a difference in disease treatment, public health, and scientific discovery.

The **Francis Crick Institute**, a leading biomedical research center based in London, has been at the forefront of studying complex diseases like cancer and infectious diseases. By partnering with AlphaProteo, the Crick Institute is able to apply its world-class expertise in biological research to test the AI-designed protein binders in laboratory settings. In the case of **SARS-CoV-2**, the virus responsible for COVID-19, the Crick Institute played a pivotal role in testing the protein binders that AlphaProteo designed to target the virus's spike protein. These tests provided essential validation, confirming that AlphaProteo's designs were not only theoretically sound but also effective in real-world scenarios. The collaboration allowed the institute to confirm that the binders were able to block the virus from infecting cells, an important milestone in the development of new therapeutics.

Beyond COVID-19, the partnership with the Crick Institute extends to other areas of critical biomedical research, including the study of cancer and autoimmune diseases. For example, in cancer research, the Crick Institute has worked with AlphaProteo to explore how protein binders designed to target proteins like V GFA, which promotes tumor angiogenesis, could be applied to experimental cancer treatments. By conducting tests in highly controlled laboratory environments, the Crick Institute's researchers have provided vital feedback on how these binders interact with cancer cells, helping to refine AlphaProteo's designs and accelerate the path from concept to clinical trials.

Collaboration with research groups like the Crick Institute not only ensures the scientific validity of AlphaProteo's designed proteins but also accelerates the process of applying these innovations to real-world medical challenges. These partnerships enable the AI system's theoretical designs to be tested under laboratory conditions, bridging the gap between AI-driven simulations and practical, life-saving treatments. The close collaboration allows for iterative improvements—if initial binders do not perform as expected in the lab, AlphaProteo can quickly redesign them based on feedback, creating an adaptive and dynamic process of scientific discovery.

In addition to the Crick Institute, AlphaProteo has partnered with other leading research groups globally, from university research labs to private institutions focused on drug development and disease research. These collaborations are essential for scaling the impact of AlphaProteo's technology. One such collaboration is with **Isomorphic Labs**, a company dedicated to using AI for drug design and development. Isomorphic Labs works closely with AlphaProteo to explore the AI's potential in creating novel treatments for a wide array of diseases. Together, they are developing new methodologies for accelerating drug discovery, where AlphaProteo's speed and precision can be leveraged to cut down the years-long timelines typically associated with pharmaceutical development.

Research groups in biotechnology and agriculture have also partnered with AlphaProteo to explore how its protein design capabilities can be applied to improve crop resilience and combat plant diseases. In this context, AlphaProteo's collaborations focus on designing proteins that enhance the ability of crops to withstand pests and environmental stressors, such as drought and extreme temperatures. By working with agricultural research institutions, AlphaProteo is extending its impact beyond human health, contributing to solutions that address global challenges like food security and environmental sustainability.

These collaborative efforts have not only validated AlphaProteo's technology but have also demonstrated its adaptability across various fields of scientific research. From designing treatments for human diseases to improving agricultural practices, the partnerships between AlphaProteo and leading research institutions are unlocking new possibilities for scientific innovation. These collaborations ensure that AlphaProteo's innovations are not confined to the theoretical realm but are tested, refined, and applied to the most pressing issues in medicine, public health, and sustainability.

Moreover, the partnerships are driven by a shared commitment to **ethical and responsible research**. AlphaProteo's developers, alongside their collaborators, are acutely aware of the power and potential risks associated with AI-designed proteins. To this end, they have worked with organizations like the **Nuclear Threat Initiative** to develop best practices for the safe and ethical use of AI in biological research. This commitment ensures that AlphaProteo's technology is directed towards positive and beneficial outcomes, with safeguards in place to prevent misuse.

AlphaProteo's collaborations with the **Francis Crick Institute** and other research groups are vital in transforming AI-designed proteins from innovative concepts into practical applications.

These partnerships not only validate the AI's groundbreaking designs but also help accelerate the development of new treatments for diseases, improve agricultural practices, and ensure that the powerful potential of AI-driven protein design is harnessed for the greater good.

As the power of artificial intelligence expands in the realm of biology, particularly with technologies like AlphaProteo, ethical considerations and biocurity measures are becoming increasingly important. AI-driven biology holds enormous potential for good, from revolutionizing medical treatments to improving agricultural resilience. However, with such advancements come risks that need to be carefully managed. Ensuring the safe and responsible use of AI-designed proteins is essential to avoid unintended consequences and prevent misuse, especially when it comes to sensitive areas like drug development, synthetic biology, and biological security.

One of the key ethical concerns surrounding AI-driven biology is the possibility of creating proteins or other biological materials that could be misused for harmful purposes. AlphaProteo's ability to design new proteins tailored to specific functions—such as neutralizing viruses or influencing immune responses—could, in theory, be repurposed for less benign uses if it fell into the wrong hands. For instance, while AlphaProteo is currently focused on designing proteins to combat diseases like COVID-19, the same technology could be exploited to create harmful biological agents or weapons if not carefully controlled.

Recognizing these risks, AlphaProteo and its development team have placed a strong emphasis on **biocurity**—the measures and protocols aimed at preventing the misuse of biological research and ensuring that all AI-designed proteins are used for positive and legitimate purposes. AlphaProteo's creators are working closely with **international organizations and security groups**, such as the

Nuclear Threat Initiative, to develop best practices for safeguarding this powerful technology. These collaborations are focused on establishing clear guidelines for the responsible use of AI in biology, ensuring that all research and applications are transparent, regulated, and monitored.

One of the fundamental steps AlphaProteo has taken in addressing ethical concerns is to establish **access controls and oversight**. While the technology's capabilities are made available to scientists and researchers, its use is closely monitored to ensure that the applications align with the original intent of promoting health, scientific advancement, and environmental sustainability. For instance, any use of AlphaProteo's AI engine for designing proteins that could be applied in sensitive or high-risk areas is subject to strict scrutiny. This includes ensuring that all users are accredited and that their research is guided by ethical standards that prioritize safety and positive outcomes.

AlphaProteo is also at the forefront of setting global best practices by promoting **open collaboration with regulatory bodies** and **international research communities**. This level of transparency is critical to ensuring that the technology is used responsibly. By working with government agencies, ethical review boards, and leading research institutions, AlphaProteo is helping to shape a framework for the responsible development and deployment of AI in biology. This involves creating **ethical review protocols** that evaluate the potential risks and benefits of AI-designed proteins before they are used in any real-world application, whether in medicine, agriculture, or industrial biotechnology.

A core element of AlphaProteo's biocurity strategy is to ensure that all AI-designed proteins undergo rigorous testing and validation before they are applied in practical settings. This helps to mitigate the risk of unintended consequences, such as off-target effects or harmful biological interactions that could arise from newly designed proteins. For instance, while AlphaProteo has successfully designed protein binders to combat viruses and diseases, each binder must be carefully tested in laboratory environments to ensure that it interacts with biological systems in a safe and predictable manner. These safeguards are essential in preventing unforeseen side effects or disruptions to natural biological processes.

Moreover, AlphaProteo is committed to addressing the broader societal implications of AI-driven biology. This includes recognizing the potential for inequality in access to these advanced technologies. AI-designed proteins have the potential to revolutionize healthcare and agriculture, but only if they are made accessible to populations across the globe, particularly in low-income and underserved regions. To this end, AlphaProteo's development team advocates for equitable distribution of AI-driven innovations, working to ensure that the benefits of this powerful technology reach beyond well-funded institutions and wealthier nations.

Another important aspect of AlphaProteo's ethical framework is the focus on **sustainability** and the **environmental impact** of AI-driven biological research. As protein design becomes increasingly integral to fields like agriculture, it is essential that the technology is used to support sustainable practices, such as reducing reliance on harmful pesticides or improving the nutritional content of crops. AlphaProteo's creators are mindful of the potential ecological consequences of introducing newly designed proteins into natural systems, and they are working to ensure that all applications align with environmental conservation efforts.

AlphaProteo's dedication to promoting responsible use extends to continuous **education and awareness** efforts. By engaging with the scientific community, policymakers, and the public, AlphaProteo aims to foster a culture of responsibility around the development and application of AI in biology. This includes raising awareness about the ethical challenges associated with synthetic biology and AI, as well as highlighting the potential benefits that can be realized when these technologies are used in a safe and controlled manner.

In conclusion, AlphaProteo is not only leading the charge in AI-driven protein design but also setting a global example for how to use such powerful technology responsibly. Through collaboration with international organizations, strict oversight, ethical review protocols, and a commitment to transparency, AlphaProteo is establishing best practices that ensure biocurity and ethical integrity. By prioritizing the safe and equitable application of AI in biology, AlphaProteo is paving the way for a future where technology serves humanity's best interests while minimizing risks and unintended consequences.

Chapter 6: Orb – AI in Material Science

Orb, developed by Orbital, represents a groundbreaking advancement in the field of material science. This AI-driven model has been specifically designed to simulate and analyze materials at the atomic level, allowing scientists to explore and create new materials with unprecedented speed and accuracy. Traditionally, the process of developing advanced materials—whether for renewable energy solutions, electronics, or industrial applications—has been time-consuming and costly. Orb changes this by using artificial intelligence to simulate how atoms and molecules behave, interact, and can be manipulated, vastly speeding up the process of material design and innovation.

At its core, Orb is an AI model tailored to simulate the intricate and complex interactions between atoms and molecules in various materials. These simulations are crucial for understanding how materials conduct energy, respond to stress, or exhibit properties such as durability, flexibility, or conductivity. The potential applications are vast, ranging from creating more efficient batteries and solar panels to improving semiconductors and developing stronger, lighter materials for manufacturing.

What sets Orb apart from traditional methods of material simulation is its ability to deliver results at a fraction of the time and with greater precision. Simulating material behavior using conventional techniques typically involves simplifying complex atomic interactions, which can lead to less accurate predictions. Moreover, these methods can take weeks or even months to provide results. Orb, on the other hand, uses AI to process vast amounts of data and perform detailed simulations in mere minutes, enabling scientists to rapidly test and refine new materials before moving on to physical experiments.

Orb's application in material science is particularly relevant in today's world, where the demand for sustainable energy solutions is higher than ever. As the world transitions toward renewable energy, the need for more efficient and longer-lasting materials is critical. Whether it's creating better batteries for electric vehicles, enhancing the efficiency of solar panels, or developing advanced materials for electronics, Orb is playing a pivotal role in driving these innovations forward.

Developed from an internal AI model called Linus, Orb has been fine-tuned specifically for material simulation. Orbital's team spent years refining this model, training it on enormous datasets of atomic structures and interactions to ensure that it could accurately predict how new materials would behave in real-world conditions. The result is a tool that not only delivers faster results but does so with a level of precision that outperforms traditional simulation models, even those created by tech giants like Google and Microsoft.

One of the most exciting aspects of Orb is its open-source availability for non-commercial use. This means that startups, researchers, and smaller labs without access to large-scale resources can utilize this cutting-edge technology to drive their own innovations. By democratizing access to such a powerful tool, Orb is helping to accelerate material science research on a global scale, fostering collaboration and breakthroughs in energy, manufacturing, and beyond.

In summary, Orb is redefining how materials are simulated and designed. With its advanced AI engine, it offers a faster, more precise way to explore the atomic behavior of materials, making it possible to create more efficient, sustainable solutions across various industries. Whether it's developing the next generation of batteries, enhancing renewable energy technologies, or driving innovation in electronics, Orb's impact is already being felt, and its potential is only beginning to unfold.

Orb is a transformative tool in material science, particularly when it comes to simulating and designing materials at the atomic level. This capability is crucial for innovations in renewable energy, battery technology, and solar panels, as these fields depend on materials that can efficiently conduct energy, store power, and withstand the rigors of long-term use. Traditionally, developing these materials required years of trial and error, with researchers slowly iterating through different compositions and configurations in labs. Orb, however, accelerates this process by simulating the precise behavior of atoms and molecules in these materials, allowing scientists to test and refine designs in a virtual environment before physical production.

At the heart of Orb's strength is its ability to predict how atoms and molecules interact with one another in a material. Every material—whether it's a conductor in a battery or a layer in a solar panel—has a specific atomic structure that determines its properties, such as conductivity, durability, and flexibility. Orb's AI model processes immense datasets of known atomic interactions, allowing it to simulate how small changes in atomic arrangements could lead to major shifts in material performance. This means that rather than manually testing each possible variation in a lab, researchers can rely on Orb to predict which configurations are likely to work best, saving both time and resources.

In the context of **renewable energy**, Orb's atomic-level simulations are critical. For example, in **solar panels**, materials must not only efficiently capture and convert sunlight into electricity but also endure harsh environmental conditions, such as intense heat, moisture, and UV exposure. By simulating different materials at the atomic level, Orb can help identify which combinations will yield the best performance in terms of energy conversion efficiency and long-term durability. This leads to faster advancements in solar technology, making solar panels more efficient and cost-effective, which is essential as the world shifts towards sustainable energy sources.

Battery technology is another area where Orb's atomic simulations are pushing the boundaries of innovation. Batteries, particularly those used in electric vehicles and renewable energy storage, require materials that can store energy efficiently, charge quickly, and last through many cycles of charging and discharging without degrading. The challenge lies in finding materials that can balance these competing demands. Orb allows researchers to simulate how different materials perform at the atomic level within battery cells, predicting how well they will store and release energy and how long they will last under real-world conditions. This ability to simulate atomic behavior helps accelerate the discovery of new battery materials that could offer higher energy density, faster charging times, and longer lifespans—critical advancements for electric vehicles and large-scale renewable energy storage solutions.

Beyond renewable energy and batteries, Orb's impact extends to broader fields such as **electronics** and **semiconductors**, where material innovation is equally crucial. As the demand for faster, more efficient, and environmentally friendly technologies grows, Orb provides the tools needed to develop next-generation materials that can meet these needs while minimizing environmental impact.

The importance of **material science** in the broader context of the **energy transition** and **environmental sustainability** cannot be overstated. As the world grapples with the urgent need to reduce reliance on fossil fuels and transition to cleaner energy sources, the development of more efficient and sustainable materials becomes critical. Whether it's through improving the efficiency of solar panels, enabling longer-lasting batteries for electric vehicles, or creating materials that reduce waste in industrial processes, advancements in material science are at the core of this transformation.

Orb's ability to simulate materials at the atomic level plays a key role in this transition. By rapidly advancing our understanding of how materials can be optimized for energy efficiency and durability, Orb is helping to create the building blocks of a sustainable energy future. **Renewable energy technologies**, such as solar panels and wind turbines, depend on materials that can operate reliably over long periods and in harsh environments. With Orb, scientists can design materials that are not only more efficient but also more environmentally friendly, reducing the need for rare or toxic elements and promoting the use of more abundant, sustainable materials.

In **energy storage**, one of the most pressing challenges is finding materials that can efficiently store and release energy from renewable sources, such as wind and solar, which do not produce energy continuously. Orb's simulations help address this by enabling the design of better battery materials that can store renewable energy for longer periods and release it when needed, thereby stabilizing the energy supply and supporting the wider adoption of renewable energy systems.

Moreover, Orb contributes to **environmental sustainability** by helping to reduce the environmental footprint of material production itself. Traditional material development often involves high energy consumption, waste, and the use of harmful chemicals. Orb's simulations allow researchers to experiment with new materials in a virtual space, cutting down on the need for physical prototypes and reducing the associated environmental costs. By optimizing material performance in a virtual environment, Orb minimizes waste, accelerates the innovation process, and supports the creation of greener technologies.

In conclusion, Orb's ability to simulate materials at the atomic level is driving key innovations in renewable energy, battery technology, and solar panels. These advancements are crucial for the global energy transition, as they enable the development of more efficient, durable, and sustainable materials that are essential for reducing our reliance on fossil fuels. Orb not only accelerates the pace of material discovery but also plays a critical role in promoting environmental sustainability, making it an invaluable tool in the quest for a cleaner, greener future.

Chapter 7: Orb's Cutting-Edge Simulation – How It Works

Orb's inner workings are a result of sophisticated AI engineering, designed specifically for the complex field of material simulation. The foundation of Orb is built upon an advanced model known as **Linus**, which was initially developed by Orbital for broader AI applications. Linus was designed to process large datasets and extract intricate patterns from complex systems, and Orb takes this further by fine-tuning Linus specifically for simulating materials at the atomic level. The modifications made to the Linus model allow Orb to excel in handling the detailed and nuanced interactions between atoms and molecules, which are critical for understanding material properties and behavior.

The core strength of Orb lies in its ability to **simulate atomic interactions** with unparalleled precision. Material behavior, such as conductivity, tensile strength, and energy storage capacity, all stem from how atoms and molecules are arranged and interact with one another. Orb's finely tuned AI algorithms process enormous amounts of data on these atomic interactions, learning how small changes in molecular structure can lead to significant shifts in material properties. This ability to predict these interactions at such a granular level is what enables Orb to simulate and optimize materials far more quickly and accurately than traditional methods.

One of the standout features of Orb is its **speed advantage**, which is up to **five times faster** than traditional material simulation techniques. Traditional methods often rely on simplified models that compromise on accuracy to make the simulations manageable. These approaches require substantial computing power and time—sometimes weeks or months—to produce results. In contrast, Orb harnesses the power of machine learning and AI to process and simulate data at lightning speeds, delivering results in hours or even minutes. This reduction in simulation time allows researchers to iterate more quickly, testing different material configurations without the long delays that typically accompany each round of physical testing.

Orb's speed advantage comes from its ability to efficiently manage vast datasets and perform parallel computations, which means it can simulate multiple scenarios simultaneously. This allows scientists to test different combinations of material properties without having to run each one sequentially, as they would with traditional methods. By processing these simulations in parallel, Orb is able to quickly narrow down the most promising material candidates, significantly reducing the time required to bring new materials from concept to reality.

Accuracy is another key area where Orb outperforms traditional simulation models and even its competitors, such as Google and Microsoft, who have also developed AI systems for material science. While Google and Microsoft have made advancements in AI-driven simulations, Orb distinguishes itself by combining speed with superior accuracy. Traditional methods often sacrifice some level of precision to reduce computation time, but Orb manages to maintain a high degree of accuracy in its predictions due to the depth of its training and the fine-tuning of its AI model. Orb's simulations are able to capture the full complexity of atomic interactions, providing results that closely mimic real-world material behavior.

This superior accuracy is due to the **Linus model's fine-tuning** for material-specific applications. Linus, while a powerful general AI model, needed significant adjustment to handle the intricate demands of material science. Orb's developers focused on optimizing the model to understand how atomic structures influence material properties at a fundamental level, improving its ability to simulate not just basic interactions but the complex and dynamic behaviors that occur under different conditions, such as heat, pressure, and electrical current.

By fine-tuning the Linus model specifically for material simulations, Orb outperforms other AI-driven models not only in speed but also in the quality of its predictions. This ability to balance speed with precision makes Orb an invaluable tool in industries where materials must be designed and tested quickly without sacrificing accuracy. For example, in renewable energy, materials must be highly efficient, durable, and capable of functioning in harsh environments. Orb's simulations allow researchers to identify materials that can meet these criteria without the lengthy trial-and-error process of traditional methods.

Moreover, Orb's **machine learning algorithms** continue to improve over time. As the model runs more simulations and gathers more data, it refines its understanding of how materials behave, making its future predictions even more accurate. This constant improvement loop allows Orb to stay ahead of competitors like Google and Microsoft, who may not have optimized their models specifically for material science to the same degree.

In conclusion, Orb's inner workings, based on the Linus model, have been carefully refined to offer superior speed and accuracy in material simulations. Its ability to simulate atomic interactions at five times the speed of traditional methods, combined with its precise predictions, allows it to outperform competitors in the field. Orb is redefining material science by providing researchers with a tool that not only accelerates discovery but also ensures that the materials they design are optimized for real-world applications, from renewable energy solutions to advanced manufacturing techniques.

Orb's advanced material simulation capabilities are having a transformative impact on the design of better batteries, improving energy efficiency, and reducing costs across multiple industries. By simulating the behavior of materials at the atomic level, Orb allows scientists to design and test new materials faster and more accurately than ever before. This ability is particularly crucial in the fields of energy storage, renewable energy solutions, and industrial applications, where advancements in materials directly lead to improvements in performance, efficiency, and cost savings.

Designing better batteries is one of the most significant applications of Orb's technology. Batteries, especially those used in electric vehicles and renewable energy storage systems, require materials that are highly efficient in storing and releasing energy, can withstand numerous charge and discharge cycles, and operate safely under various conditions. Traditionally, the development of new battery materials involved years of experimentation, with researchers having to manually test different combinations of materials to identify those that offer better energy density, faster charging times, and longer lifespans.

Orb streamlines this process by simulating the performance of battery materials at the atomic level before they are physically tested. This enables researchers to explore a vast range of material combinations virtually, identifying the most promising candidates much faster than traditional methods. For instance, in **lithium-ion batteries**, Orb can simulate how different cathode and anode materials interact with lithium ions, predicting how well the materials will perform in terms of energy storage capacity and stability over time. By identifying materials that have higher energy densities and are less prone to degradation, Orb helps create batteries that can last longer and store more energy in a smaller, lighter package.

This has profound implications for the electric vehicle industry, where the demand for longer-range, faster-charging, and more durable batteries is a top priority. Orb's simulations can help identify materials that reduce the amount of time it takes to charge a battery while improving its overall lifespan, making electric vehicles more practical and appealing to consumers. Additionally, better battery design leads to reductions in the weight and size of batteries, which can improve vehicle efficiency and reduce manufacturing costs.

In the context of **renewable energy**, Orb's material simulations are also critical for improving the performance of batteries used to store energy generated from sources like solar and wind. Renewable energy systems often face the challenge of intermittent generation—solar panels, for example, only produce energy when the sun is shining. Efficient energy storage solutions are needed to store this energy for use when it is not being generated. Orb allows researchers to design advanced battery materials that can store more energy for longer periods and release it efficiently when needed, supporting a more stable and reliable energy supply.

Beyond batteries, Orb plays a key role in **improving energy efficiency** in various systems and devices. Whether it's improving the thermal conductivity of materials used in electronic devices or designing materials that reduce energy loss in power transmission systems, Orb helps optimize the materials that underpin energy-efficient technologies. In electronic devices, for instance, heat dissipation is a major concern. Poorly designed materials can trap heat, reducing device efficiency and shortening their operational lifespan. Orb's simulations can predict which materials will offer better heat conduction, improving device performance while using less energy.

In **solar panels**, Orb's simulations enable the discovery of new materials that are more efficient at converting sunlight into electricity. By identifying materials that can better absorb and conduct solar energy, Orb helps create solar panels with higher conversion rates, meaning they can produce more electricity from the same amount of sunlight. This improvement in efficiency can reduce the overall cost of solar energy systems, making renewable energy more affordable and accessible to a broader range of consumers.

Cost reduction is another significant benefit of using Orb in material design. By simulating materials before they are produced, Orb reduces the need for costly and time-consuming physical experiments. Researchers can quickly rule out materials that are unlikely to perform well, focusing only on the most promising candidates for real-world testing. This ability to narrow down options early in the design process leads to faster development cycles and lower research and development costs.

Additionally, Orb enables the discovery of materials that are more abundant or easier to source, which can further reduce manufacturing costs. For instance, many advanced batteries rely on rare or expensive materials, such as cobalt, which drive up costs and create supply chain vulnerabilities. Orb can help identify alternative materials that offer similar or even better performance at a lower cost, reducing dependence on scarce resources and promoting the use of more sustainable, easily sourced materials.

In summary, Orb's applications in **battery design**, **energy efficiency**, and **cost reduction** are reshaping industries by enabling the rapid development of advanced materials that perform better, last longer, and cost less to produce. Whether it's creating batteries that support the global shift toward electric vehicles and renewable energy or designing more efficient materials for electronic devices and industrial processes, Orb is driving innovation that promises to have a lasting impact on both the economy and the environment.

Chapter 8: Open Source Power – Orb's Potential for Innovation

Orb's decision to be open-source for non-commercial use is a strategic and impactful move that reflects its commitment to democratizing access to advanced AI tools. By making this powerful material simulation model available to a wide audience—particularly researchers, startups, and institutions without the resources of large corporations—Orbital is ensuring that innovation in material science is not limited to a few well-funded players. Instead, it fosters a more inclusive environment where a broader range of scientists and engineers can leverage cutting-edge technology to drive discoveries and advancements across industries.

One of the primary reasons Orb is open-source for non-commercial use is to **accelerate scientific**

research. Material science plays a critical role in solving some of the world's most pressing challenges, from developing more efficient energy storage systems to designing sustainable materials for manufacturing and construction. However, access to advanced AI tools like Orb has historically been restricted to well-funded organizations that can afford the high costs of proprietary software and the infrastructure required to run complex simulations. By offering Orb's technology to the broader scientific community for free, Orbital is empowering smaller research groups and universities to conduct high-level material simulations that would otherwise be out of reach.

This **democratization of access** to Orb's technology is particularly important in the context of addressing global issues such as climate change, where advancements in energy storage, renewable energy, and sustainable materials are urgently needed. Smaller research labs, particularly those in developing countries, often face financial and technical barriers that limit their ability to contribute to cutting-edge research. Orb's open-source model allows these groups to harness the same tools as large corporations and research institutions, leveling the playing field and fostering innovation from diverse corners of the world.

By providing free access to Orb for non-commercial purposes, Orbital is also promoting **collaboration and knowledge-sharing**. Open-source models encourage the exchange of ideas, data, and methods among scientists and engineers. As more researchers use Orb to simulate materials and share their findings, the collective knowledge base around material science grows. This collaborative approach accelerates the pace of discovery, as breakthroughs made by one group can be built upon by others, driving the field forward more quickly than if each group worked in isolation. In this way, Orb's open-source availability not only broadens access to its tools but also creates a network effect, where innovation feeds on itself and progresses more rapidly.

Additionally, making Orb open-source for non-commercial use is a way for Orbital to **contribute to the broader scientific community** and ensure that the benefits of AI-driven research are shared widely. While proprietary AI models can generate significant revenue for companies, they can also limit who can access and benefit from the technology. Orbital's decision to open up Orb reflects a commitment to the idea that certain innovations—especially those with the potential to address global challenges—should be accessible to all, not just to those with the financial means. This philosophy aligns with the broader trends in the AI and tech communities, where open-source models like TensorFlow and PyTorch have driven innovation by providing free access to sophisticated tools.

Moreover, making Orb open-source for non-commercial purposes encourages

experimentation and innovation beyond what might occur in traditional corporate research settings. Startups, university labs, and independent researchers are often able to take risks and explore unconventional ideas that might not be prioritized by larger organizations focused on short-term commercial gains. By giving these smaller players access to powerful AI tools like Orb, Orbital is enabling them to explore novel approaches to material science, potentially leading to breakthroughs that would otherwise remain undiscovered.

For example, in the field of **renewable energy**, a small research lab using Orb could design new materials for more efficient solar panels or more durable batteries, contributing to global sustainability efforts. Similarly, startups focused on **sustainable manufacturing** could use Orb to discover materials that reduce waste and lower environmental impact. By removing the cost barrier, Orbital is facilitating the development of solutions that might otherwise be delayed or ignored due to financial constraints.

Finally, Orb's open-source model for non-commercial use acts as a **springboard for commercial innovation** down the line. By allowing researchers and startups to use Orb for free during the initial, experimental phases of their work, Orbital is helping them prove the viability of new materials and processes. Once these innovations reach a point where they can be commercialized, users can transition to Orb's commercial licensing model, generating value for both the researchers and Orbital. This approach fosters a **win-win scenario** where early-stage innovation is supported, and successful breakthroughs can eventually translate into commercial applications and business growth.

In conclusion, Orb's open-source availability for non-commercial use is a powerful tool for democratizing access to advanced AI technology, fostering collaboration, and accelerating innovation in material science. By removing the barriers that traditionally limit access to such sophisticated tools, Orbital is ensuring that a wide range of researchers, startups, and institutions can contribute to solving global challenges. This open-access model not only drives innovation but also builds a more inclusive, collaborative, and forward-thinking scientific community.

Startups and researchers are finding new ways to drive innovation in material sciences through Orb's advanced simulation capabilities. The ability to quickly test and refine materials at the atomic level allows them to innovate faster and more efficiently than traditional methods. For startups, where resources are often limited, this offers a critical advantage. Instead of spending time and money on physical experiments and prototypes, they can simulate how materials will behave under different conditions, reducing the cost and time needed to bring new ideas to market.

Researchers are also leveraging Orb to conduct high-level experiments in areas like energy storage, sustainable materials, and advanced manufacturing. This AI-driven tool allows them to explore material properties in ways that were previously too costly or technically challenging. In battery technology, for example, startups are using Orb to develop new materials that enhance energy density, charge more quickly, and offer longer life spans. Orb allows them to simulate different material combinations, optimizing designs for better performance without the delays of traditional lab testing. In solar energy, researchers are using Orb to identify more efficient photovoltaic materials, pushing the boundaries of renewable energy by improving the conversion rates of solar panels.

A notable success story comes from a startup working on solid-state batteries. By utilizing Orb's simulations, they were able to design a new type of solid electrolyte that addresses key challenges in energy storage, such as safety and performance. This innovation attracted the attention of major automotive companies looking to improve the range and reliability of electric vehicles. The speed at which they developed this breakthrough—much faster than would have been possible through conventional methods—demonstrates Orb's impact on the energy sector.

Another example involves a research group focused on organic solar cells. Using Orb, they were able to simulate and optimize different organic compounds to improve the efficiency of solar energy conversion. This work has advanced the technology significantly, moving it closer to commercialization and expanding the potential applications for flexible, lightweight solar panels in various industries.

Looking ahead, the future of Orb is full of possibilities. Orbital, the company behind this AI tool, is continually refining and expanding its capabilities. With plans to integrate quantum computing techniques, Orb will be able to simulate even more complex materials with greater accuracy. This next step in its evolution could unlock entirely new areas of research, allowing startups and researchers to push further into advanced material design. Additionally, Orbital is exploring partnerships with major industry players to apply Orb's capabilities in large-scale commercial projects, from aerospace to energy infrastructure.

With more tools and features expected to be added to the open-source platform, Orb is set to play a growing role in democratizing access to cutting-edge material science. Researchers and startups, regardless of their size or funding, will continue to use Orb to innovate faster and more efficiently, contributing to technological advancements that are both groundbreaking and sustainable. As it evolves, Orb is poised to remain at the forefront of material science innovation, making a lasting impact on industries and the global shift toward more efficient, sustainable technologies.

Chapter 9: The Bigger Picture – AI's Role in the Future of Science

AI models like AlphaProteo and Orb are driving broader scientific advancements by accelerating research, improving precision, and opening up new frontiers in various fields. Both models use the power of artificial intelligence to tackle complex scientific challenges that have traditionally been limited by time, cost, and human capacity. By automating and optimizing tasks that once required labor-intensive processes, these AI systems are not only increasing the speed of discovery but also enabling breakthroughs that would have been difficult or impossible to achieve through conventional means.

AlphaProteo is contributing to advancements in biology and medicine by designing new proteins that can be tailored to target specific molecules, making it a valuable tool for drug discovery and therapeutic development. The ability to create custom protein binders that can neutralize disease-causing agents, such as viruses or cancer-related proteins, has revolutionized the approach to treating complex diseases. Where traditional methods of drug design could take years to yield results, AlphaProteo accelerates the process by generating highly effective protein designs in a fraction of the time. Its impact is particularly evident in fields like oncology and infectious disease research, where it has already demonstrated success in creating binders for cancer-related proteins and viral spike proteins such as those found in SARS-CoV-2. This leap in capability is helping scientists to develop more targeted treatments with greater efficiency, offering hope for new therapies in areas where traditional approaches have struggled.

Meanwhile, Orb is contributing to advancements in material science by simulating the behavior of materials at the atomic level. This capability allows scientists to explore new materials and optimize existing ones for use in energy storage, electronics, and other high-performance applications. Orb's AI-driven simulations are particularly valuable in the renewable energy sector, where the demand for better materials in batteries and solar panels is critical for advancing sustainable technologies. The ability to simulate how materials will perform under different conditions—whether in batteries that need to store more energy or solar panels that need to convert sunlight more efficiently—means that researchers can quickly iterate on designs, speeding up the development process and reducing the cost of experimentation. Orb is not just limited to energy applications; it is also helping to improve materials used in aerospace, automotive, and industrial manufacturing, where the need for lightweight, durable, and high-performance materials is constantly evolving.

Both AlphaProteo and Orb are part of a broader movement in science where AI is being integrated into research to address complex problems that were previously limited by traditional methodologies. AI models like these are making it possible to process vast amounts of data and identify patterns that humans might miss, uncovering new insights and solutions in fields ranging from medicine to materials science. As these models evolve, they will likely continue to contribute to scientific advancements in other areas, such as agriculture, environmental science, and biotechnology.

The broader impact of AI-driven research models is that they are democratizing science by making advanced tools accessible to more researchers, regardless of their resources. This means that smaller labs and startups can now compete on a level playing field with larger institutions, driving innovation from diverse sources. By accelerating the pace of discovery and enhancing the precision of scientific work, AI models like AlphaProteo and Orb are not only advancing their respective fields but also shaping the future of science as a whole. The ripple effect of these advancements is being felt across industries, leading to more sustainable, efficient, and innovative technologies that are poised to address some of the world's most pressing challenges.

The future of AI in drug discovery, material design, and energy solutions is incredibly promising, as these technologies continue to push the boundaries of what is possible in science and industry. AI models like AlphaProteo and Orb are already demonstrating their capacity to accelerate breakthroughs, and as they evolve, their impact on these fields is expected to grow even further.

In **drug discovery**, AI is poised to transform the way new treatments are developed. Traditional drug discovery is a lengthy and expensive process, often taking years to move from initial research to clinical trials. AI models like AlphaProteo are speeding up this process by designing new proteins and molecules that target disease-causing agents with precision. The ability to simulate how these molecules interact with specific proteins allows researchers to test multiple drug candidates in a short period of time, drastically reducing the time it takes to develop new therapies. The future of AI in drug discovery lies in its potential to personalize medicine even further, tailoring treatments to individual patients based on their genetic makeup and the specific characteristics of their disease. As AI becomes more advanced, it will likely be able to predict side effects and efficacy more accurately, resulting in safer and more effective treatments.

In **material design**, AI models like Orb are reshaping the development of new materials by simulating their properties at the atomic level. The materials that are critical to industries such as energy, electronics, and aerospace can be designed and tested in virtual environments, allowing researchers to optimize their performance before they are physically produced. The future of AI in this field involves not only creating materials that are stronger, lighter, and more durable but also designing materials that are more sustainable and environmentally friendly. As AI continues to evolve, it will play a vital role in advancing technologies such as **quantum computing**, **nanomaterials**, and **biomaterials**, opening new possibilities for innovation across multiple sectors.

Energy solutions are another area where AI is set to have a transformative impact. The demand for renewable energy sources is growing rapidly as the world seeks to reduce its reliance on fossil fuels. AI can optimize energy storage systems, improve the efficiency of solar and wind technologies, and contribute to the development of smart grids that manage energy distribution more effectively. By simulating materials that can store and convert energy more efficiently, AI models like Orb are helping to advance battery technology and renewable energy systems, making them more viable for large-scale adoption. The future of AI in energy lies in its ability to integrate renewable sources into a cohesive, resilient energy network that can meet the world's growing energy needs while minimizing environmental impact.

The potential for **cross-industry collaborations** to unlock even more of AI's potential in global innovation is vast. AI's strengths in pattern recognition, simulation, and optimization make it a valuable tool across industries, and when sectors such as healthcare, energy, and materials science collaborate, the synergies created can lead to breakthrough innovations. For instance, collaborations between pharmaceutical companies and tech firms specializing in AI could lead to faster drug development cycles, with better predictions of drug interactions and efficacy. Similarly, partnerships between energy companies and material science researchers can result in the creation of more efficient solar panels or batteries, powered by AI simulations that optimize both materials and energy systems.

These **cross-industry collaborations** could also accelerate the development of technologies that address pressing global challenges, such as climate change and public health. For example, AI's ability to predict material behaviors could support the development of carbon capture technologies or create new biodegradable materials that reduce environmental waste. Likewise, collaborations between AI researchers and medical institutions could lead to advancements in medical diagnostics, allowing for earlier detection of diseases and more effective preventive care.

As AI continues to evolve, the opportunities for collaboration between industries will expand. AI models can bridge gaps between sectors, bringing together expertise from diverse fields to tackle complex problems that require interdisciplinary solutions. Whether it's using AI to design new materials for energy-efficient buildings, applying

AI-driven simulations to optimize manufacturing processes, or leveraging AI in drug development to combat pandemics, the future of AI is one of interconnected innovation. These collaborative efforts have the potential to unlock unprecedented advances in technology, improving the quality of life and addressing global challenges in ways that were previously unimaginable.

In conclusion, the future of AI in drug discovery, material design, and energy solutions is bright, with the potential for cross-industry collaborations to further unlock its global potential. As AI continues to evolve, it will play a central role in driving innovation across industries, enabling faster, more efficient, and more sustainable solutions to some of the world's most complex problems. This future will be shaped by the ability of different sectors to work together, harnessing the power of AI to build a more advanced, interconnected, and sustainable world.

Conclusion

As we look ahead to the future shaped by AI-driven advancements, the impact of models like AlphaProteo and Orb becomes increasingly clear. These cutting-edge technologies are not only revolutionizing how we approach drug discovery and material design but also expanding the limits of what's achievable in medicine, energy, and numerous other fields. The journey from their research inception to real-world applications is a testament to the power of artificial intelligence as a transformative tool, accelerating scientific progress and bringing new solutions to some of the world's most pressing challenges.

AlphaProteo has already demonstrated its value in reshaping the landscape of protein design, offering new avenues for targeted therapies in diseases like cancer, autoimmune disorders, and viral infections. By designing proteins that bind to specific disease-causing molecules, AlphaProteo has greatly reduced the time and cost traditionally associated with drug discovery, making the development of new treatments more accessible and efficient. In the coming years, its influence on personalized medicine and therapeutic innovations will only deepen, potentially leading to breakthroughs that improve the quality of healthcare globally.

Similarly, Orb is propelling material science into the future by enabling the simulation of materials at the atomic level. Its ability to predict how materials will behave under various conditions is streamlining the creation of more efficient, durable, and sustainable solutions. Whether it's in renewable energy, advanced manufacturing, or electronic design, Orb is catalyzing faster development cycles and enabling innovations that have the potential to reshape industries. The success stories of startups and researchers already using Orb to optimize energy storage and solar technologies are just the beginning of its broader impact on global innovation.

As these technologies continue to evolve, the responsibility of guiding AI advancements with an ethical framework becomes ever more critical. While the possibilities unlocked by AI are immense, they come with the obligation to ensure that these tools are used responsibly, equitably, and for the greater good. AlphaProteo and Orb are setting global best practices by promoting collaboration, transparency, and security in their applications, demonstrating a commitment to advancing science while safeguarding against potential risks.

The ethical considerations surrounding AI-driven biology and material science, particularly regarding biocurity, environmental impact, and access to technology, will remain at the forefront of ongoing developments. It will be essential to strike a balance between pushing the boundaries of innovation and ensuring that these advancements benefit society as a whole. The collaboration between researchers, industry leaders, and policymakers will play a key role in maintaining this balance, ensuring that AI is used to solve global challenges in a way that is both ethical and sustainable.

In conclusion, AlphaProteo and Orb represent the cutting edge of AI's potential in medicine, science, and technology. Their journey from research labs to real-world applications highlights the transformative power of AI, offering faster, more precise, and more efficient solutions to complex problems. As we continue to unlock new possibilities through AI, the focus must remain on using these advancements to benefit humanity responsibly. The future of AI is bright, filled with opportunities to create a more connected, innovative, and sustainable world, but it is up to us to guide that future with care and foresight.

www.ingramcontent.com/pod-product-compliance
Lightning Source LLC
LaVergne TN
LVHW051711050326
832903LV00032B/4148

9 7 9 8 3 3 8 8 0 1 4 6 8